A Note From Rick Renner

I am on a personal quest to see a "revival of the Bible" so people can establish their lives on a firm foundation that will stand strong and endure the test as end-time storm winds begin to intensify.

In order to experience a revival of the Bible in your personal life, it is important to take time each day to read, receive, and apply its truths to your life. James tells us that if we will continue in the perfect law of liberty — refusing to be forgetful hearers, but determined to be doers — we will be blessed in our ways. As you watch or listen to the programs in this series and work through this corresponding study guide, I trust you will search the Scriptures and allow the Holy Spirit to help you hear something new from God's Word that applies specifically to your life. I encourage you to be a doer of the Word He reveals to you. Whatever the cost, I assure you — it will be worth it.

> Thy words were found, and I did eat them;
> and thy word was unto me the joy and rejoicing of mine heart:
> for I am called by thy name, O Lord God of hosts.
> — Jeremiah 15:16

Your brother and friend in Jesus Christ,

Rick Renner

What To Do When You're Being Bombarded

Copyright © 2021 by Rick Renner
P.O. Box 702040
Tulsa, OK 74170

Published by Rick Renner Ministries
www.renner.org

ISBN 13: 978-1-68031-949-1

eBook ISBN 13: 978-1-68031-950-7

How To Use This Study Guide

This five-lesson study guide corresponds to *"What To Do When You're Being Bombarded" With Rick Renner* (Renner TV). Each lesson in this study guide covers a topic that is addressed during the program series, with questions and references supplied to draw you deeper into your own private study of the Scriptures on this subject.

To derive the most benefit from this study guide, consider the following:

First, watch or listen to the program prior to working through the corresponding lesson in this guide. (Programs can also be viewed at **renner.org** by clicking on the Media/Archives links.)

Second, take the time to look up the scriptures included in each lesson. Prayerfully consider their application to your own life.

Third, use a journal or notebook to make note of your answers to each lesson's Study Questions and Practical Application challenges.

Fourth, invest specific time in prayer and in the Word of God to consult with the Holy Spirit. Write down the scriptures or insights He reveals to you.

Finally, take action! Whatever the Lord tells you to do according to His Word, do it.

For added insights on this subject, it is recommended that you obtain Rick Renner's books *Dressed To Kill: A Biblical Approach to Spiritual Warfare and Armor* and Rick and Denise's autobiography *Unlikely: Our Faith-Filled Journey to the Ends of the Earth.* You may also select from Rick's other available resources by placing your order at **renner.org** or by calling 1-800-742-5593.

TOPIC

What Triggers an Attack?

SCRIPTURES

1. **2 Timothy 1:9-12** — Who hath saved us, and called us with an holy calling, not according to our works, but according to his own purpose and grace, which was given us in Christ Jesus before the world began, but is now made manifest by the appearing of our Saviour Jesus Christ, who hath abolished death, and hath brought life and immortality to light through the gospel: whereunto I am appointed a preacher, and an apostle, and a teacher of the Gentiles. For the which cause I also suffer these things: nevertheless I am not ashamed: for I know whom I have believed, and am persuaded that he is able to keep that which I have committed unto him against that day.

2. **2 Corinthians 12:7** — And lest I should be exalted above measure through the abundance of the revelations, there was given to me a thorn in the flesh, the messenger of Satan to buffet me, lest I should be exalted above measure.

GREEK WORDS

1. "suffer" — πάσχω (*pasho*): I suffer; emotional suffering; strong feelings

2. "ashamed" — ἐπαισχύνομαι (*epaishunomai*): disgraced; put to shame; embarrassed; red-faced

3. "I know" — οἶδα (*oida*): to see, perceive, understand, or comprehend; knowledge gained by personal experience or personal observation

4. "persuaded" — πείθω (*peitho*): one who is convinced, coaxed, or swayed from one opinion to the opinion held by another; absolute confidence; convinced to the core; rock-solid certainty

5. "able" — δυνατός (*dunatos*): ability; power; a powerful force; amazing ability; to be able; capable or competent for any task; a force that causes one to be able or capable; one who is competent

6. "keep" — φυλάσσω (*phulasso*): to save, protect, preserve, or guard; a military guard who shows uninterrupted vigilance in guarding

territory; the uninterrupted vigilance shepherds show in keeping their flocks

7. "committed" — παραθήκη (*paratheke*): entrust; deposit; commit into one's charge or trust for safekeeping

8. "exalted above measure" — ὑπεραίρω (*huperairo*): a compound of the words ὑπέρ (*huper*) and αἴρω (*airo*); the word ὑπέρ (*huper*) means over, above, and beyond; depicts something that is way beyond measure and conveys the idea of something that is greater, superior, higher, better, more than a match for, utmost, paramount, or foremost; describes something that is first-rate, first-class, top-notch, unsurpassed, unequaled, and unrivaled by any person or thing; the word αἴρω (*airo*) means to lift up, to raise, or to be exalted; when compounded, a person who has been supremely exalted; one who has been magnified, increased, and lifted up to a place of great influence

9. "thorn" — σκόλοψ (*skolops*): a dangerously sharp, spiked instrument or tool; also used to describe the stake on which an enemy's head was stuck after being decapitated

10. "buffet" — κολαφίζω (*kolaphidzo*): from a word that describes the fist or knuckles; here it refers to beatings with the fist; the Greek tense describes unending, unrelenting, continuous, repetitious beatings

SYNOPSIS

The five lessons in this study on *What To Do When You're Being Bombarded* will focus on the following topics:

- What Triggers an Attack?
- Attacks Against Your Finances
- Attacks Against Your Marriage
- Attacks Against Your Children or Grandchildren
- Attacks Against Your Health

The emphasis of this lesson:

One of the primary reasons the devil attacks you as a believer is to distract you and ultimately derail you from your God-ordained assignment. That's why Satan continually attacked the apostle Paul and even assigned a demonic envoy to repeatedly harass and assault him in every

city he went. But God's grace showed up every time and kept Paul safe from Satan's plans.

The city of Saint Petersburg, Russia, has had a number of names throughout its history. First it was called Saint Petersburg, then it was renamed Petrograd, and after that it was called Leningrad. Today, it is once again called Saint Petersburg.

But back in 1941, something horrific began to take place in this city. It is referred to as the siege of Leningrad. It was at that time that Nazi troops surrounded the city in order to take it captive. Much to their surprise, the people of Leningrad dug in their heels, defended their city, and refused to give up.

To pressure the residents, the Nazis cut off all supplies going into the city. When the people ran out of food, they began to eat cats, dogs, and rats. As the situation worsened, they began eating wallpaper, wallpaper paste, and even paint. In desperation, they turned to cooking their leather shoes and belts for food. Through it all, they refused to surrender to the attacking forces.

History reveals that at least 1.5 million residents died of starvation and from the freezing temperatures. During that particular time, the temperatures fell to minus 40. Sadly, more than a million soviet troops perished in the defense of the city. Today, historians estimate that about 3 million people died over the 900 days surrounding the siege. It is documented that at one period of time the local morgues in Saint Petersburg were cremating 8,800 people a day.

In spite of all the extreme hardships, the spirit of the city remained strong and refused to surrender to the attack. But why did the attack take place? Why did the Nazis want Leningrad so intensely? The answer is because it was a very important city filled with history and great treasures.

This brings us to the all-important question: What triggers attacks in your life? Why does the devil come after you? That, friend, is the reason for this series and what we will focus on for the next five lessons.

Paul Revealed the Cause for His Suffering

If there was anyone who understood what it meant to be under attack, it was the apostle Paul. By the time he came to the latter part of his ministry, he was able to grasp why the devil was attacking him so fiercely. In Second Timothy 1:9-12 he said:

> [God] Who hath saved us, and called us with an holy calling, not according to our works, but according to his own purpose and grace, which was given us in Christ Jesus before the world began, but is now made manifest by the appearing of our Saviour Jesus Christ, who hath abolished death, and hath brought life and immortality to light through the gospel:
>
> Whereunto I am appointed a preacher, and an apostle, and a teacher of the Gentiles. For the which cause I also suffer these things: nevertheless I am not ashamed: for I know whom I have believed, and am persuaded that he is able to keep that which I have committed unto him against that day.

In this passage, Paul cites clearly the reason for all the suffering he was going through. In verse 12, he says, "For the which cause I also suffer these things...." What was the cause? It was *the call of God on his life*. He defined that call in verse 11, saying, "Whereunto I am appointed a preacher, and an apostle, and a teacher of the Gentiles."

Essentially, Paul said, "If you want to know why I'm going through everything I'm going through, it's because the devil is after my calling. I've been appointed a preacher, an apostle, and a teacher of the Gentiles, and because I've become such a threat to the domain of darkness, I'm suffering these things."

Nero Concocted an Evil Scheme Against the Christians in Rome

It is interesting to note that the word "suffer" in verse 12 is the Greek word *pasho*, which means *to physically suffer* or *to emotionally suffer*. It can also describe *strong feelings*. At this particular moment in Paul's life, he had been arrested and confined to a Roman prison for a crime he didn't commit.

At that time, Nero was the Roman emperor, and he had decided that he wanted to build himself a new palace in the heart of Rome. The problem was there were many notable buildings standing in the place he wanted to erect his palace. Accordingly, he requested permission from the Roman senate to tear them down, but they denied his request because of the area's rich historic value.

It has been said by many historians that Nero circumvented this roadblock by ordering his servants to set fire to the buildings in question. Indeed, an intense inferno raged throughout the city for several days. Eventually, the fire was finally brought under control, but not without significant loss and devastation to the city of Rome.

When the smoke cleared, it became apparent that the area where Nero wanted to build his home was now totally cleared. Hence, he began construction of his new palace. The Roman senate quickly came to the conclusion that Nero himself was the instigator of the fire because of his personal desire to build his new palace. For that reason, formal charges were brought against him.

However, as they were bringing him to the senate for his trial and execution, he concocted an evil scheme to defend himself. As Nero stood before the senate, his argument must have sounded something like this: "How could you even think that I, Nero, would burn down my own city that I love so much? I would never do such a thing. But I'll tell you who did it." And the senate said, "Yes, tell us who did this dastardly deed."

"It was that new group in town that we've been hearing on our street corners," Nero declared. "It's those Christians that have been preaching to us and publically saying that a terrible day of judgment is coming that would be marked with fire and brimstone. We should've listened to them. Obviously, they were sending us a secret message that they were going to burn down the city of Rome, which is exactly what they've done."

Sadly, without any significant investigation to corroborate Nero's story, the Roman senate believed him, and that is when the first official governmental persecution of Christians began. Although there had been prior religious persecution, this was the first governmental-sponsored persecution against Christians.

Paul Was Imprisoned on False Charges

Suddenly, Christians began to be rounded up and arrested. Some were killed and others were imprisoned. During the process, a list was made of those that were believed to be the most visible Christian leaders — and, of course, Paul's name was on that list. In fact, it was at the very top. And because he was such a visible Christian leader, certain Roman officials alleged that he was one of the arsonist's that planned the fire that burned down the central section of Rome.

Consequently, Paul was arrested and imprisoned in Rome. It was from his prison cell that he wrote the book of Second Timothy. To clarify, he was not in prison because he was a Christian; he was in prison because he was charged with being an arsonist.

Keep in mind, very few things were worse than being in a Roman prison. In fact, Roman prisons were so horrifying that most prisoners never left, but died there. For that reason, they rarely even fed these prisoners because they were considered to be useless eaters that were going to die anyway.

There Paul was, living in a dark, damp, hideous dungeon with little food of which to speak. It seems the whole world was talking about him, and the narrative of the Roman press basically stated that Paul was the man who helped plan the fire that burned down the city of Rome.

Undoubtedly, as Paul was sitting in prison and all this fake news was being circulated throughout the city of Rome, there were people who were calling for his death. His name became notorious for a crime he didn't commit. Paul — and many others — were taking the blame for Nero's wrongdoing, and he was suffering in prison as a result.

Paul Was 'Persuaded' of God's Unrivaled Ability

Immediately after Paul identified the call of God on His life and pointed to it as the reason he was suffering, he went on to make this remarkable declaration:

> **...Nevertheless I am not ashamed: for I know whom I have believed, and am persuaded that he is able to keep that which I have committed unto him against that day.**
> **— 2 Timothy 1:12**

There are several key words in this verse that deserve our attention. The first one is the word "ashamed." It is the Greek word *epaishunomai*, which means *to be disgraced, put to shame, embarrassed,* or *to be red-faced.* In spite of everything that was being said about Paul, he was not disgraced or embarrassed. Even though he was in prison, he was not ashamed. Why? He said, "…For I know whom I have believed…" (2 Timothy 1:12).

In Greek, the phrase "I know" is a translation of the word *oida*, which means *to see, perceive, understand, or comprehend*. It describes *knowledge gained by personal experience* or *personal observation*. Paul had personally experienced the Person and power of Jesus Christ, and as a result he said, "…[I] am persuaded that he is able…" (2 Timothy 1:12). The word "persuaded" here is the Greek word *peitho*, and it describes *one who is convinced, coaxed, or swayed from one opinion to the opinion held by another*. This is a person who has *absolute confidence* and is *convinced to the core* with *rock-solid certainty*.

The use of this word *peitho* ("persuaded") tells us that while Paul was suffering in prison, he had moments when he may have been tempted to be fearful or worry about what would happen. Therefore, he did a lot of self-talk. That is what this word *peitho* can describe — *self-persuasion*. Sometimes when we're in trouble, we need to talk to ourselves and remind ourselves of who God is and what He's done in our lives. We have to push back against the devil's lies and turn a deaf ear to our emotions. If we're not careful, both can deceive us and put us into a state of panic.

Paul talked to himself in that dark, dank prison and had coaxed and convinced himself that God was "…able to keep that which [he had] committed unto him against that day" (2 Timothy 1:12).

God Is 'Able To Keep' Us!

The word "able" in Second Timothy 1:12 is the Greek word *dunatos*, and it describes *ability, power,* or *a powerful force*. It denotes *amazing ability* and means *to be able, capable or competent for any task*. Paul's use of this word demonstrates his belief that God is *a force that was well-able or capable and competent* to "keep" him.

This word "keep," translated from the Greek word *phulasso*, means *to save, protect, preserve, or guard*. It denotes *a military guard who shows uninterrupted vigilance in guarding territory*. It is also the word used to depict *the uninterrupted vigilance shepherds show in keeping their flocks*. By using this word, Paul was saying, "I am persuaded and convinced that God is able — *fully competent* and *capable* — to keep me with uninterrupted vigilance. He's protecting and guarding and watching over me much like a shepherd keeps uninterrupted vigilance over his sheep."

What is God able to keep? Paul said, "…That which I have committed unto him against that day" (2 Timothy 1:12). The word "committed" here is the Greek word *paratheke*, and it means *to entrust* or *to deposit; to commit into one's charge or trust for safekeeping.*

One of the best illustrations of this word *paratheke* ("committed") is the act of making a night deposit at a bank. Usually somewhere on the bank building, especially in times past, is a large, metal door that is connected to a safety deposit container in the bank. To make a deposit, you pull down the thick metal door and slip your envelope into the small horizontal opening. Once the door is pushed closed, the deposit is safely secured inside the bank and cannot be touched or tampered with in any way.

Similarly, when a person gives his life to Christ, he effectively deposits himself *in Christ* and out of the enemy's reach. The moment he or she is *in Christ*, nothing and no one can tamper with or touch them. This is what the apostle Paul was saying — and he was making this declaration of faith from a Roman prison cell of all places. He believed beyond the shadow of a doubt that God was able to keep him until "that day," which refers to the day we see Jesus face-to-face and our mission here is completed.

The Enemy Attacked Paul Because of His Place of Great Influence

So what is it that often triggers an attack in our lives? To help get an even greater handle on the cause let's look at Paul's words in Second Corinthians 12:7. Here the apostle tells us, "And lest I should be exalted above measure through the abundance of the revelations, there was given to me a thorn in the flesh, the messenger of Satan to buffet me, lest I should be exalted above measure."

Now there have been various interpretations of what Paul is saying here. Some have gone so far as to say God Himself sent Paul trials and troubles because he had become proud and conceited because of the many revelations he had been given. But was that really the case?

One of the keys to understanding the meaning of this verse is found in the phrase "exalted above measure." In Greek, this is the word *huperairo*, a compound of the words *huper* and *airo*. The word *huper* means *over, above, and beyond* and depicts *something that is way beyond measure.* It conveys the idea of something that is *greater, superior, higher, better, more than a match for, utmost, paramount,* or *foremost.* It describes something that is *first-rate, first-class, top-notch, unsurpassed, unequaled,* and *unrivaled by any person or thing.* And the word *airo* means *to lift up, to raise,* or *to be exalted.*

When the words *huper* and *airo* are compounded, it depicts *a person who has been supremely exalted* or *one who has been magnified, increased, and lifted up to a place of great influence.* With this understanding, we can see that Paul was saying, "As a result of all the vast revelations God has given me, I have been raised to a position of great influence that few people possess. And because of these revelations and the impact I'm making, there was given to me a thorn in the flesh...."

The fact that Paul said the thorn was *given* to him, often causes people to automatically assume it was given to him from God. But that is not what the verse says. Rather, it says that the thorn in the flesh was "the messenger of Satan." Thus, a better translation would be, "...There was assigned unto me a thorn in the flesh...."

Now this word "thorn" has been the topic of much discussion in the Church. In Greek, it is the word *skolops,* which describes *a dangerously sharp, spiked instrument or tool.* What's interesting is that this word was also used to describe *the stake on which an enemy's head was stuck after being decapitated.* By using this word *skolops* — translated here as "thorn" — Paul was literally saying, "I am making such advancements with the Gospel and my position has become so exalted and influential that the devil is after me and he wants my head on a stake!"

Notice that Paul calls this thorn "the messenger of Satan." Satan had sent out one of his demons to "buffet" Paul. That word "buffet" is the Greek word *kolaphidzo,* which is from a word that describes *the fist* or *knuckles.* Here it refers to *beatings with the fist,* and the Greek tense indicates *unending, unrelenting, continuous, repetitious beatings.* This was Paul's "thorn in the flesh" — a demonic attack sent out by Satan himself to relentlessly and continuously beat and attack Paul in order to derail him from his God-ordained purpose.

Taking into account the original Greek meaning of these key words, here is the *Renner Interpretive Version (RIV)* of Second Corinthians 12:7:

> **Because of the phenomenal revelations I have received and on account of the vast number of these revelations that God has entrusted to me — and to hinder the highly visible progress I**

am making — a special messenger has been sent from Satan to harass me with constant distractions and headaches. There's no doubt about it! Satan wants my head on a stake! Satan is constantly trying to buffet and distract me in an attempt to keep me from reaching a higher level of visibility and recognition and to sidetrack me from preaching my revelations.

In our next lesson, we will continue our study on what we are to do when we're being bombarded, and see what else Paul revealed in his candid letters to his spiritual son Timothy.

STUDY QUESTIONS

Study to shew thyself approved unto God, a workman that needeth not to be ashamed, rightly dividing the word of truth.
— 2 Timothy 2:15

1. What new details did you learn about Paul's life in this lesson? How about Nero's connection with Paul's arrest and imprisonment? Why did Paul say he was suffering?

2. In the midst of a ghastly Roman prison cell, Paul talked to himself and persuaded himself that God was well-able to guard, protect, and preserve him until he saw Jesus face to face. What does God say about His *keeping power* and *delivering power* in your life in these verses?

   • **Isaiah 43:2 and Joshua 1:7-9**

   • **Hebrews 7:24,25**

   • **2 Peter 2:9 and 2 Timothy 4:18**

   • **Jude 24 and Psalm 121:1-8**

3. What did Jesus Himself say about His care and the Father's care of you in John 10:27-30? How do these words from your Good Shepherd comfort and encourage you?

PRACTICAL APPLICATION

But be ye doers of the word, and not hearers only, deceiving your own selves.
— James 1:22

1. Prior to this lesson, had you ever heard of Paul's "thorn in the flesh" (see 2 Corinthians 12:7)? If so, what did you understand his thorn to be? How has this lesson helped you see this verse more clearly and even help clear up any misconceptions about God's character?

2. Are there any particular people that the devil uses regularly to bring grief and frustration in your life? In what ways are they like a "thorn" in your flesh? How do their actions irritate you or distract you from your calling?

3. Take time now to pray and ask the Lord for a divine strategy in dealing with these "enemies" and for practical steps you can take to strengthen yourself to stay focused and on task with what God has assigned you to do.

LESSON 2

TOPIC

Attacks Against Your Finances

SCRIPTURES

1. **2 Timothy 1:11-14** — Whereunto I am appointed a preacher, and an apostle, and a teacher of the Gentiles. For the which cause I also suffer these things: nevertheless I am not ashamed: for I know whom I have believed, and am persuaded that he is able to keep that which I have committed unto him against that day. Hold fast the form of sound words, which thou hast heard of me, in faith and love which is in Christ Jesus. That good thing which was committed unto thee keep by the Holy Ghost which dwelleth in us.

2. **Hebrews 10:32** — But call to remembrance the former days, in which, after ye were illuminated, ye endured a great fight of afflictions.

3. **1 John 5:4** — For whatsoever is born of God overcometh the world: and this is the victory that overcometh the world, even our faith.

GREEK WORDS

1. "suffer" — **πάσχω** (*pasho*): I suffer; emotional suffering; strong feelings

2. "ashamed" — **ἐπαισχύνομαι** (*epaishunomai*): disgraced; put to shame; embarrassed; red-faced

3. "I know" — **οἶδα** (*oida*): to see, perceive, understand, or comprehend; knowledge gained by personal experience or personal observation

4. "persuaded" — **πείθω** (*peitho*): one who is convinced, coaxed, or swayed from one opinion to the opinion held by another; absolute confidence; convinced to the core; rock-solid certainty

5. "able" — **δυνατός** (*dunatos*): ability; power; a powerful force; amazing ability; to be able; capable or competent for any task; a force that causes one to be able or capable; one who is competent

6. "keep" — **φυλάσσω** (*phulasso*): to save, protect, preserve, or guard; a military guard who shows uninterrupted vigilance in guarding territory; the uninterrupted vigilance shepherds show in keeping their flocks

7. "committed" — **παραθήκη** (*paratheke*): entrust; deposit; commit into one's charge or trust for safekeeping

8. "hold fast" — **ἔχε** (*eche*): to have, hold, retain, possess

9. "form" — **ὑποτύπωσις** (*hupotoposis*): compound of **ὑπό** (*hupo*) and **τύπος** (*tupos*); the word **ὑπό** (*hupo*) means by and the word **τύπος** (*tupos*) means a model or pattern; denotes a model forged by repetition; a pattern to be followed and repeated

10. "sound" — **ὑγιαίνω** (*hugiaino*): indicates something that is wholesome and healthy and that produces a healthy state of being

11. "illuminated" — **φωτίζω** (*photidzo*): to illuminate; gives the impression of a brilliant flash of light that leaves a permanent and lasting impression

12. "endured" — **ὑπομένω** (*hupomeno*): to stay or abide; to remain in one's spot; to keep a position; to resolve to maintain territory gained; in a military sense, it pictures soldiers ordered to maintain their positions even in the face of opposition; to defiantly stick it out regardless of pressures mounted against it; staying power; hang-in-there power; the attitude that holds out, holds on, outlasts, perseveres, and hangs in there, never giving up, refusing to surrender to obstacles, and turning down every opportunity to quit; pictures one who is under a heavy load but refuses to bend, break, or surrender because he is convinced that the territory, promise, or principle under assault rightfully belongs to him

SYNOPSIS

In 1941, Nazi troops surrounded the city of Leningrad, Russia, and attempted to starve the people into submission. Leningrad was a very important city in the Soviet Union, and the Nazis wanted to seize it for their own strategic purposes. But the people of Leningrad refused to surrender. Their spirit simply would not be dominated by their enemy.

So for 900 days, they held their ground and resisted the Nazi's attack. During that time, food and supplies only came into the city in very small quantities. In fact, there was so little food that people resorted to eating anything they could get their hands on, including their dogs, their cats, their birds, and even rats. When those things ran out, they resorted to cooking anything they had that was made out of leather, such as their belts and shoes. Once that supply was exhausted, they began eating the wallpaper and paint.

Adding to the food shortage was extremely harsh weather conditions. At one point during the standoff, the temperatures dropped to 40 degrees below zero, and as you can imagine, many people began to die simply because of the freezing temperatures. Indeed, it was a dreadful and indescribable 900 days. But finally, at the end of a stretch of time, the siege was over, and there was great victory in Leningrad because the citizens had outlasted the attack.

In our last lesson, we learned that sometimes we are attacked by Satan because of the call of God on our lives. Likewise, we also come under assault just after our hearts and minds have been illuminated by truth. That is what the writer of Hebrews pointed out in his letter to the Hebrew believers. He said, "But call to remembrance the former days, in which, after ye were illuminated, ye endured a great fight of afflictions" (Hebrews 10:32).

Maybe you've been under assault and you've wondered why. Well, when you've been illuminated with truth, you become a greater threat to the enemy, and he counters with an attack against you to nullify and steal that illumination.

The emphasis of this lesson:

Immediately after you've received an eye-opening revelation of truth from God, the enemy turns up the heat against you. This is especially

true in the area of your finances. When you're illuminated to the importance and blessing of giving tithes and offerings and you begin to give, Satan often attacks your finances. But if you'll refuse to surrender and continue giving, you'll outlast the enemy, and abundant blessings will begin to flow!

A REVIEW OF OUR ANCHOR VERSE
2 Timothy 1:12

When Paul wrote his second letter to his young apprentice Timothy, Paul was suffering in a Roman prison for a crime he didn't commit. He and many other Christians had been falsely accused by the Roman Emperor Nero and the Roman senate of the crime of setting fire to the central section of the city of Rome.

Paul said, "For the which cause I also suffer these things…" (2 Timothy 1:12). The cause for his suffering is found in the previous verse where he said, "Whereunto I am appointed a preacher, and an apostle, and a teacher of the Gentiles" (2 Timothy 1:11). Paul knew God's call on his life, and he was wholeheartedly giving himself to that call and making tremendous progress. It was because of the anointing on his life to be a preacher, an apostle, and a teacher of the Gentiles that he was targeted by Nero and thrown in prison to "suffer."

This word "suffer" in Second Timothy 1:12 is the Greek word *pasho*, which means *to physically suffer* or *emotionally suffer*. It was Paul's calling that caused him to be arrested and thrown into prison. Yet, Paul went on to declare:

> …Nevertheless I am not ashamed: for I know whom I have believed, and am persuaded that he is able to keep that which I have committed unto him against that day.
> — 2 Timothy 1:12

Paul was not "ashamed." The word "ashamed" here is the Greek word *epaishunomai*, which means *to be disgraced, put to shame, or embarrassed*. In fact, this is a person so embarrassed their face is turning red. In Paul's case, he was *not* disgraced, embarrassed, or red in the face. Even though he was in prison and being lied about by the Roman officials, he was not ashamed. Why? Because he knew who he was, and he knew in whom he was believing.

Paul said, "…For I know whom I have believed…" (2 Timothy 1:12). In Greek, the phrase "I know" is the word *oida*, which means *to see, perceive, understand, or comprehend.* It describes *knowledge gained by personal experience* or *personal observation.* By this point in Paul's life, he had extensive personal experience with God and knew that God would come through and help him in whatever situations he faced.

Paul said, "…[I] am persuaded…" (2 Timothy 1:12). The word "persuaded" in this verse is the Greek word *peitho*, and it describes *one who is convinced, coaxed, or swayed from one opinion to the opinion held by another.* The fact that Paul said, "I am persuaded (*peitho*)," tells us that while Paul was suffering in prison, he had to deal with his rogue thoughts and feelings. He likely experienced times when he was tempted to be fearful or worry about what was going to happen.

Instead of giving in to fear and unbelief, he began talking to himself, coaxing and convincing himself that God had not left him and that everything was going to work out. That is what this word *peitho* is describing here — *self-persuasion.* Paul had talked to himself and persuaded himself to stay in a place of faith long enough that he was able to develop *absolute confidence* and be *convinced to the core* with *rock-solid certainty* that God was able to keep him.

Paul said, "…He is able to keep…" (2 Timothy 1:12). The word "able" here is the Greek word *dunatos*, and it describes *ability, power,* or *a powerful force.* It denotes *amazing ability* and means *to be able, capable or competent for any task.* By using this word "keep" (*dunatos*), Paul was saying, "God is absolutely *competent* and *capable* to 'keep' me through this extremely difficult situation."

The word "keep" in Greek is *phulasso*, and it means *to save, protect, preserve, or guard.* Thus, Paul was saying, "God is well-able to save me, protect me, preserve me, and guard me." This word *phulasso* — translated here as "keep" — was also the word used to denote *a military guard who employed uninterrupted vigilance in guarding territory.* Moreover, it depicted *the uninterrupted vigilance shepherds show in keeping their flocks.* By using this word, Paul was saying, "I am God's territory — I am God's sheep. I am fully convinced that He is competent and capable to watch over me with uninterrupted vigilance; He will protect me, preserve me, and save me."

What is God able to keep? Paul said, "…That which I have committed unto him against that day" (2 Timothy 1:12). Here, the word "that" refers to Paul himself. And the word "committed" is the Greek word *paratheke*, which means *to entrust* or *to deposit*; *to commit into one's charge or trust for safekeeping*. It is as if Paul is comparing himself to money placed into a night depository at a bank. Once that deposit is placed into the small open door and the door is pushed closed, the deposit is safely secured inside the bank and cannot be touched or tampered with in any way.

Essentially, Paul was saying, "I've entrusted my life to Jesus. I've deposited myself into His care and keeping. No one can touch me or harm me. I am *in Christ* forever, and He is able to keep me until that day." The words "that day" refer to the day we see Jesus face to face and our mission here is completed.

Timothy Was Battling Fear

Keep in mind that the reason Paul was writing Timothy is because he also was being attacked, and we know one of the weapons the enemy was bringing against Timothy was *fear*. As many things came against Timothy from many angles, he was being tempted to give into a spirit of fear.

That's why Paul reminded him just moments earlier, "For God hath not given us the spirit of fear; but of power, and of love, and of a sound mind" (2 Timothy 1:7). The Greek word for "fear" here describes *a spirit of cowardice*. It's a demonic spirit that makes you *cower* and *hide*.

When a spirit of fear is operating in your life, you don't have a sound mind. A fearful spirit produces thinking that is irrational and full of panic. The longer you give place to a spirit of fear, the more you begin to worry about everything. Fear begins to fill your imagination so strongly that you begin to worry about totally irrational things that will never happen to you. To an unsound mind, even the absurd seems real.

That's why Paul reminded Timothy, "Hey Timothy, God has not given you a spirit that makes you a coward — or so afraid that you run and hide. Rather, God has given you His Spirit of power and of love and of a sound mind."

Paul Urged Timothy
To Get a Grip on His Mouth

Paul went on to tell Timothy, "Hold fast the form of sound words, which thou hast heard of me, in faith and love which is in Christ Jesus" (2 Timothy 1:13). The words "hold fast" are from the Greek word *eche*, which means *to have, hold, retain, or possess*. Paul was urging Timothy to hold tightly to and retain possession of "the form of sound words."

In Greek, the word "form" is *hupotoposis*, which is a compound of the words *hupo* and *tupos*. The word *hupo* means *by*, and the word *tupos* describes *a model* or *pattern*. Specifically, *tupos* denotes *a model forged by repetition*; *a pattern to be followed and repeated*. Paul told Timothy to work hard at holding on to the pattern of "sound words" Paul had modeled in front of him. The word "sound" here is the Greek word *hugiaino*, and it indicates *something that is wholesome and healthy and that produces a healthy state of being*.

At the time of the writing of this second letter to Timothy, both Paul and Timothy were being attacked. And while Paul was in faith and fully persuaded of God's keeping power, Timothy was fighting against the spirit of fear. In this moment, Paul told Timothy, "Hold fast the form of sound words, which thou hast heard of me…" (2 Timothy 1:13). In other words, Paul said, "Timothy, stick with and follow the pattern of sound words, which you heard from me."

This tells us that Paul had a regular pattern of speaking, and it was so steady and consistent that others like Timothy were familiar with it. Basically, Paul was telling Timothy, "When you're tempted to give into fear, get a firm grip on your mouth. Speak *sound* words, not negative or fearful words. Talk about what is wholesome and healthy and what will produce a healthy state of being. Follow the pattern of speech you heard from me, and speak words of faith and love which are in Christ Jesus."

Please understand that when you are being attacked, you need to speak words of *faith* and not fear. If you speak negative words of fear and unbelief, you will cooperate with what the spirit of fear is trying to do in your life. On the other hand, when you speak *sound* words of faith, you will be cooperating with the Holy Spirit, repelling the enemy's attack and preserving a sound mind.

Save, Protect, and Guard
What God Has Entrusted to You

Continuing his instruction to Timothy, Paul added, "That good thing which was committed unto thee keep by the Holy Ghost which dwelleth in us" (2 Timothy 1:14). What is the "good thing" Paul is telling Timothy to keep? It is the God-ordained calling on his life — it is the spiritual gift and the Spirit's anointing that empowers the gift. It is all the revelation of truth God has deposited in his spirit.

Paul told Timothy to keep these things by the enabling power of the Holy Spirit that "dwelleth in us." The word "dwelleth" here means *to take up permanent residence*. Thus, the Holy Spirit becomes a *permanent resident* in you the day you surrender your life to the lordship of Jesus. That means you're not alone! You have a supernatural partner — the Holy Spirit — living on the inside of you! He's empowering you to do everything you need to do — which includes "keeping" all the good things He's committed to you.

The word "keep" in Second Timothy 1:14 is again the Greek word *phulasso*, and it means *to save, protect, preserve, or guard*. It depicts *a military guard who shows uninterrupted vigilance in guarding territory*, and it also denotes *the uninterrupted vigilance shepherds show in keeping their flocks*.

Isn't that interesting? God promises to "keep" (*phulasso*) us — *to save, protect, preserve, and guard* us with *uninterrupted vigilance*. And at the same time, He commands us to "keep" (*phulasso*) — *to save, protect, preserve, and guard* with *uninterrupted vigilance* — what He's entrusted to us. Again, this includes His calling on our life, His anointing, and the revelation of truth He has given us.

Enemy Attacks Often Follow
Moments of Illumination

As we noted in the introduction, the enemy often attacks us just after our hearts and minds have been illuminated by truth. That's what the writer of Hebrews points out in his letter to the Hebrew believers. He said, "But call to remembrance the former days, in which, after ye were illuminated, ye endured a great fight of afflictions" (Hebrews 10:32).

The word "illuminated" in this verse is the Greek word *photidzo*, and it means *to illuminate*. It is from where we get the word *photograph*, and it describes *a brilliant flash of light that leaves a permanent and lasting impression.* This word *photidzo*, translated here "illuminated," denotes any and all moments when the Holy Spirit of God gives you spiritual eyes to see truth that you have never seen before. This revelation is so powerful and impactful that it leaves a permanent impression on you.

Now the interesting thing about a moment of illumination is that the writer of Hebrews says, "…After ye were illuminated, ye endured a great fight of afflictions" (Hebrews 10:32). In other words, a spiritual fight often follows illumination. A fresh revelation of truth often triggers trials and troubles from the enemy. Why? Because Satan despises people who are illuminated; they are a major threat to his kingdom of darkness.

God Has Called Us To 'Endure'

When these Hebrew believers were attacked by the enemy, the Bible says they "endured." This word "endured" is a form of the Greek word *hupomeno*, which means *to stay* or *abide*; *to remain in one's spot, to keep a position,* or *to resolve to maintain territory gained.* In a military sense, it pictures *soldiers ordered to maintain their positions even in the face of opposition.* It means *to defiantly stick it out regardless of pressures mounted against it.* It is *staying power* or *hang-in-there power.* It is *the attitude that holds out, holds on, outlasts, perseveres, and hangs in there, never giving up, refusing to surrender to obstacles, and turning down every opportunity to quit.* It pictures *one who is under a heavy load but refuses to bend, break, or surrender because he is convinced that the territory, promise, or principle under assault rightfully belongs to him.*

Friend, you need to understand that after you've been illuminated — after the Holy Spirit has revealed truth to you in a powerful way — the enemy is likely going to try to get you to release the revelation you just received. For instance, if you've received illumination on the importance and blessing of obeying God through giving your tithes and offerings, the devil is going to do all he can to bring difficult circumstances into your life to wear you down and get you to let go of what you learned. And if he can get you to stop giving, he can close the windows of Heaven over your life and stop you from receiving the full harvest of financial blessing God wants to pour out

When the enemy comes against you in this way, you need to make the decision to not give in or give up on what God has revealed to you through His Word. It's not time to bend or to break. It's time to press into God's presence and *endure!* If God has illuminated you in the area of giving, refuse to surrender *the territory, promise, or principle under assault because it rightfully belongs to you!*

The good news is, eventually the enemy's attack will come to an end, and he who endures to the end always wins — always! The Early Church understood the importance and great value of learning how to endure. In fact, they called endurance *the queen of all virtues.* They knew if they could endure the enemy's attacks, it wasn't a question of IF they would win — it was a question of WHEN they would win. Endurance is the supernatural ability to outlast the enemy!

So if your finances have come under attack, first make sure you *stick with a form of sound words.* In other words, speak *faith* not fear and unbelief regarding your financial situation. Second, stay in your place of faith and *keep doing what God has told you to do.* There is an expiration date on the enemy's attack. It will come to an end, and when it does, you'll be so glad you "endured" (*hupomeno*) and stayed in your place of faith.

STUDY QUESTIONS

Study to shew thyself approved unto God, a workman that needeth not to be ashamed, rightly dividing the word of truth.
— 2 Timothy 2:15

1. One thing is clear: God is a Giver, and He has instructed all those who love Him — in Old Testament and New Testament times — to give. Carefully reflect on Malachi 3:10,11 and Second Corinthians 9:6,7 and jot down what the Holy Spirit shows you about how we are to give and the blessings we can expect Him to provide.

2. If you've stepped out in faith and started giving your tithes and offerings, the enemy is not happy. If he's attacking your finances, you may be tempted to give into fear. Now more than ever, it's vital for you to get a grip on the words from your lips! Here are some powerful promises from Scripture that you can begin to meditate on and *speak* out loud over your life:
   • **Psalm 34:6,9,10 and Psalm 84:11**

- **Luke 6:38**
- **2 Corinthians 9:8-11**
- **Philippians 4:19**
- **Romans 8:31,32**

PRACTICAL APPLICATION

> But be ye doers of the word, and not hearers only,
> deceiving your own selves.
> — James 1:22

1. Paul said, "…[God] is able to keep that which I have committed unto him against that day" (2 Timothy 1:12). The word "committed" means *to entrust* or *to deposit into one's charge for safekeeping*. The question is, have you "committed" yourself, your family, your situations, your *everything* into God's safekeeping? What have you *not* deposited and entrusted to God? Why not begin committing *all that you are* and *all that you have* into His safekeeping today and every day!

2. When Timothy was being tempted to give into fear, Paul urged him to stick with and follow the pattern of *sound, wholesome words* of faith and love which Paul had a habit of speaking. Who do you know who speaks sound, healthy words — even in the midst of trials and troubles? What kinds of words and phrases do they speak that you can begin speaking that will produce a healthy state of being in your life?

3. The word "illuminated" is the Greek word *photidzo*, and it describes *a brilliant flash of light that leaves a permanent and lasting impression.* Can you recall a "*photidzo*" moment when the Holy Spirit illuminated truth to your heart and mind? Describe what He revealed to you and how it is still impacting your life today.

4. According to Hebrews 10:32, a fresh illumination of truth often triggers an attack. Can you remember how the enemy came against you after you received revelation from God? How did the Holy Spirit bring you through it, and what is something valuable He taught you?

TOPIC
Attacks Against Your Marriage

SCRIPTURES

1. **2 Timothy 1:11-14** — Whereunto I am appointed a preacher, and an apostle, and a teacher of the Gentiles. For the which cause I also suffer these things: nevertheless I am not ashamed: for I know whom I have believed, and am persuaded that he is able to keep that which I have committed unto him against that day. Hold fast the form of sound words, which thou hast heard of me, in faith and love which is in Christ Jesus. That good thing which was committed unto thee keep by the Holy Ghost which dwelleth in us.

2. **Mark 4:37** — And there arose a great storm of wind, and the waves beat into the ship, so that it was now full.

3. **1 John 5:4** — For whatsoever is born of God overcometh the world: and this is the victory that overcometh the world, even our faith.

GREEK WORDS

1. "suffer" — πάσχω (*pasho*): I suffer; emotional suffering; strong feelings

2. "ashamed" — ἐπαισχύνομαι (*epaishunomai*): disgraced; put to shame; embarrassed; red-faced

3. "I know" — οἶδα (*oida*): to see, perceive, understand, or comprehend; knowledge gained by personal experience or personal observation

4. "persuaded" — πείθω (*peitho*): one who is convinced, coaxed, or swayed from one opinion to the opinion held by another; absolute confidence; convinced to the core; rock-solid certainty

5. "able" — δυνατός (*dunatos*): ability; power; a powerful force; amazing ability; to be able; capable or competent for any task; a force that causes one to be able or capable; one who is competent

6. "keep" — φυλάσσω (*phulasso*): to save, protect, preserve, or guard; a military guard who shows uninterrupted vigilance in guarding territory; the uninterrupted vigilance shepherds show in keeping their flocks

7. "committed" — **παραθήκη** (*paratheke*): entrust; deposit; commit into one's charge or trust for safekeeping

8. "hold fast" — **ἔχε** (*eche*): to have, hold, retain, possess

9. "form" — **ὑποτύπωσις** (*hupotoposis*): compound of **ὑπό** (*hupo*) and **τύπος** (*tupos*); the word **ὑπό** (*hupo*) means by and the word **τύπος** (*tupos*) means a model or pattern; denotes a model forged by repetition; a pattern to be followed and repeated

10. "sound" — **ὑγιαίνω** (*hugiaino*): indicates something that is wholesome and healthy and that produces a healthy state of being

11. "there arose" — **γίνομαι** (*ginomai*): to take by surprise; to take off-guard; not anticipated

12. "great" — **μεγάλη** (*megale*): great; enormous

13. "storm" — **λαῖλαψ** (*lailaps*): atmospheric turbulence

14. "wind" — **ἄνεμος** (*anemos*): a strong wind; a storm-like force

15. "waves" — **κύματα** (*kumata*): billowing waves; one wave after another; usually describes a succession of ongoing waves

16. "beat into" — **ἐπιβάλλω** (*epiballo*): to throw against; to cast over; to throw over

17. "overcometh" — **νίκη** (*nike*): to conquer; to overcome; used to portray athletes who gained the mastery in a competition and reigned supreme as champions over the games; ultimate champions; the superior position of an overcomer

18. "victory" — **νίκη** (*nike*): to conquer; to overcome; used to portray athletes who gained the mastery in a competition and reigned supreme as champions over the games; ultimate champions; the superior position of an overcomer

SYNOPSIS

If you visit the city of Saint Petersburg, Russia, today, there is a special, solemn memorial honoring the defense of Leningrad. As we have seen in our previous lessons, in 1941, Nazi troops surrounded the city in an attempt to starve its residents into surrendering. For 900 days the city was under siege, and enemy soldiers blocked virtually all food and supplies from entering.

To compensate for the shortage, the people began growing whatever they could grow in any open space available. But once winter set in, they couldn't grow anything anymore. In desperation, the people began eating anything they could get their hands on, including their dogs, cats, birds, and rats. They even cooked their leather belts and shoes and ate them in order to make it through and survive the assault.

The people of Leningrad had an invincible spirit that refused to surrender — it's the same kind of spirit we need to have when we come under attack. We need to make the decision to remain steadfast and hold tightly to what God has entrusted to us. It doesn't matter how hard the enemy bombards us or how much pressure we're under. We must decide we're not going to surrender or yield any territory that rightfully belongs to us!

For instance, if you're married, your marriage is territory God has entrusted to you. More than likely, you and your spouse started out well, but through the years things may have deteriorated. Even if your relationship appears to be hanging by a thread, you don't have to throw in the towel. Through the empowerment of the Holy Spirit, you can make the decision to stand firm and fight to maintain your marriage. Like the people of Leningrad, you will see victory when you outlast the enemy!

The emphasis of this lesson:

Marriage is a reflection of Jesus' relationship with us — His bride. That's why Satan attacks your marriage, bringing wave after wave of trouble against you and your spouse. However, if you'll stand and take authority over the devil, declaring sound words of truth over your marriage and against the enemy, it's only a matter of time until his assault ceases!

A REVIEW OF OUR ANCHOR VERSE

2 Timothy 1:12

The apostle Paul was a legendary leader in the Early Church. Yet that did not exclude him from coming under attack. The enemy came against Paul then just as he comes against us now. Therefore, we shouldn't be surprised by his assaults. If you're living to honor God and advance His Kingdom in your sphere of influence, the enemy *is* going to attack.

In Second Timothy 1:12, Paul said, "For the which cause I also suffer these things…." What was the cause of Paul's suffering? He tells us in verse 11: "Whereunto I am appointed a preacher, and an apostle, and a teacher of the Gentiles." Paul knew he was making significant progress in advancing the Gospel among the Gentiles, and for that reason, Satan was doing everything he could to stop him.

With resolve, Paul continued by declaring, "…Nevertheless I am not ashamed…" (2 Timothy 1:12). We've seen that this word "ashamed" — the Greek word *epaishunomai* — means *disgraced, put to shame, embarrassed,* or *red-faced.* Regardless of the hardships Paul was experiencing, he was not blushing with embarrassment nor was he disgraced. Why? Paul tells us in his next breath: "…For I know whom I have believed…" (2 Timothy 1:12). The words "I know" in Greek is the word *oida,* which means *to see, perceive, understand, or comprehend something based on personal experience or personal observation.* Paul had personally witnessed the power of Jesus Christ actively protecting and directing his life.

Consequently, he was able to say, "…[I] am persuaded that he is able…" (2 Timothy 1:12). The word "persuaded" here is the Greek word *peitho,* and it describes *one who is convinced, coaxed, or swayed from one opinion to the opinion held by another.* In the dreariness of his dark, damp prison cell, Paul was probably tempted to drift into doubt and negativity. But because of his personal knowledge of God and how God proved Himself to be faithful again and again, Paul was able to talk to himself and convince himself to continue to trust God in spite of how bleak his situation looked.

That's what this word "persuaded" (*peitho*) means. It describes *self-talk* that results in a person becoming *absolutely confident* and *convinced to the core* with *rock-solid certainty.* Paul used his words to *coax* and *persuade* himself to believe for the best. In this case, he convinced himself, "…that he [God] is able to keep that which I have committed unto him against that day" (2 Timothy 1:12).

The word "able" in this verse is a form of the Greek word *dunatos,* and it means *to be able, capable or competent for any task.* Paul's use of this word demonstrates that he believed God had *the amazing ability and was well-able, capable, and competent* to "keep" him.

We have seen that this word "keep" — the Greek word *phulasso* — means *to save, protect, preserve,* or *guard.* It denotes *a military guard who shows uninterrupted vigilance in guarding territory.* It also depicts *the uninterrupted vigilance shepherds show in keeping their flocks.* By using this word, Paul was basically saying, "God is my Great Soldier who's guarding me vigilantly; I am His territory. He is my Great Shepherd, and I am His sheep that He is watching over. I am fully persuaded and convinced that God is *competent* and *capable* of guarding me with uninterrupted vigilance."

What was Paul's part in all this? He said he had "committed" himself to the Lord. The word "committed" is the Greek word *paratheke*, and it means *to entrust, to deposit*, or *to commit into one's charge or trust for safekeeping.* This means Paul had *deposited* himself into the care of God, and now God was responsible to *guard*, to *protect*, and to *preserve* him. The same holds true for anything you "commit" (*paratheke*) into God's care. Whether it's your finances, your marriage, your family, or yourself, whatever you deposit with God, He will watch over, defend, and protect.

When You're Being Attacked, Speak Words of *Faith* and *Love*, Not Fear

In Second Timothy 1:13, Paul went on to tell Timothy, "Hold fast the form of sound words, which thou hast heard of me, in faith and love which is in Christ Jesus."

It is important to realize that Timothy had been around Paul most of his adult life. Therefore, he had heard how Paul spoke — including what he said in difficult, desperate situations. At this moment in time, Timothy was pastoring the large, influential church at Ephesus, and they were experiencing persecution. Personally, Timothy was being tempted to give in to a spirit of fear and begin speaking negative words. This is when Paul told him, "Hold fast the form of sound words, which thou hast heard of me…" (2 Timothy 1:13).

The phrase "hold fast" is from the Greek word *eche*, which means *to have, hold, retain, or possess.* Paul was urging Timothy to *hold tightly to* and *retain possession of* "the form of sound words." The word "form" here is the Greek word *hupotoposis,* and it denotes *a pattern to be followed and repeated again and again.* The word "sound" is the Greek word *hugiaino*, and it indicates *something that is wholesome and healthy and that produces a healthy state of being.*

This verse lets us know that Paul had a consistent pattern of speaking with which Timothy would have been familiar. Basically, Paul was telling Timothy, "Stick with and follow the pattern of sound words, which you heard me speak. I know you're tempted to give into fear, but you need to get a grip on your tongue. Speak *sound* words, not negative or fearful words. Talk about wholesome and healthy things and what will produce a healthy state of being. Follow the pattern of speech you heard from me, and speak words of *faith* and *love* which are in Christ Jesus."

Remember, when you're being attacked, you need to speak words of *faith* and not fear. If you speak negative words of fear and unbelief, you will actually be helping to bring about what the spirit of fear is trying to do in your life. On the other hand, when you speak *sound* words of faith, you will be cooperating with the Holy Spirit, repelling the enemy's attack and safeguarding a sound mind.

Turbulent Storms Often Arise Out of Nowhere

One of the areas of our lives that the enemy will often attack is our marriage. The relationship between a husband and wife is a reflection of the relationship between Jesus and us — His Church. This makes Christian marriages a prime target for satanic attack. Oftentimes, marriages start off well. Husbands love and care for their wives, and wives honor and respect their husbands. But as time passes, the exhilaration of the honeymoon fades, leaving the relationship vulnerable. Then suddenly, a storm of hurricane proportions hits the marriage and begins to beat against it fiercely.

A good illustration of this scenario is found in the fourth chapter of Mark. Here we find Jesus and His disciples crossing from one side of the Sea of Galilee to the other. The Bible says, "And there arose a great storm of wind, and the waves beat into the ship, so that it was now full" (Mark 4:37). Notice the phrase "there arose." It is a translation of the Greek word *ginomai*, which means *to take by surprise* or *to take off-guard*. This is an *unanticipated* event that takes you by surprise.

When Jesus and His disciples began their journey, it seemed to be the perfect night for sailing. The skies were clear and the weather was pleasant. But then suddenly, out of nowhere (*ginomai*), a great storm of wind arose. The word "great" here is the Greek word *megale*, and it means *great* or *enormous*. It's from where we get the word *mega*. This was a *mega* "storm." The Greek word for "storm" is *lailaps*, which describes *atmospheric turbulence*.

Does that sound familiar? Everything in your marriage is cruising along peacefully, and then suddenly you and your spouse begin to bear the brunt of major *atmospheric turbulence*. In the disciples' case, the turbulence was a serious "wind" storm. The word "wind" is the Greek word *anemos*, and it describes *a strong wind* or *a storm-like force*. This strong wind was blowing so powerfully it created "....waves [that] beat into the ship, so that it was now full" (Mark 4:37).

The word "waves" is a translation of the Greek word *kumata*, which describes *billowing waves* that are literally hitting *one wave after another*. This word usually describes *a succession of ongoing waves*, and the Bible says they "beat into the ship." The phrase "beat into" is a form of the Greek word *epiballo*, which means *to throw against, to cast over*, or *to throw over*. This word implies that there was an invisible force — a spiritual entity — picking up the waves and throwing them against the ship in an effort to deliberately swamp and capsize it. But why?

If you read ahead to Mark 5, you'll see that Jesus had spiritual business on the other side of that sea. He was about to do major damage to the kingdom of darkness by delivering the demoniac from a legion of demons (which is 6,000 in number). The devil knew where Jesus was headed, and therefore tried to stop Him from reaching His destination. But the devil failed!

In a similar way, Satan often comes against your marriage. You are heading in the right direction; God is using you and your spouse to really help change people's lives. Everything seems to be smooth sailing for a while, and then BAM! You suddenly begin to experience great *turbulence*. Strong winds begin to blow, creating great waves that smash against your marriage one after the other. It seems like wave after wave are being picked up by some invisible force and then strategically hurled at specific areas of your relationship — like your communication, your quality time together, and times of sexual intimacy. The bombardment grows so intense it appears your marriage will not survive.

That's what was happening to Jesus and His disciples on that very night. But after the disciples turned to Jesus and woke Him from his sleep, the Bible says, "And he arose, and rebuked the wind, and said unto the sea, Peace, be still. And the wind ceased, and there was a great calm" (Mark 4:39). They made it to the other side of the sea because Jesus stood up and took authority over the wind and the waves. You will make it too, if you'll stand up and take authority over the enemy — speaking words of faith and love!

Your Marriage Is a 'Good Thing' God Has Committed to You

Friend, whatever God has committed and entrusted to you — including your marriage — He wants you to keep watch over. That is what the Holy Spirit prompted Paul to write in Second Timothy 1:14. He said, "That good thing which was committed unto thee keep by the Holy Ghost which dwelleth in us" (2 Timothy 1:14). Along with the divine calling on your life and the anointing of the Holy Spirit, your marriage is another "good thing" God has committed to you.

Paul told Timothy to keep these things by the enabling power of the Holy Spirit that "dwelleth in us." Again, the word "dwelleth" here means *to take up permanent residence.* That is what the Holy Spirit does the day you surrender your life to the lordship of Jesus — He becomes a *permanent resident* inside you. That means you're not alone! You have a supernatural partner — the Holy Spirit — living inside you! He's empowering you to do everything you need to do — which includes "keeping" your marriage and every other good thing He's committed to you.

The word "keep" in Second Timothy 1:14 is the Greek word *phulasso,* and it means *to save, protect, preserve, or guard.* It depicts *a military guard who shows uninterrupted vigilance in guarding territory,* and it also denotes *the uninterrupted vigilance shepherds show in keeping their flocks.*

As we noted in our previous lesson, God promises to "keep" (*phulasso*) us — *to save, protect, preserve, and guard* us with *uninterrupted vigilance.* And at the same time, He commands us to "keep" — *to save, protect, preserve, and guard* with *uninterrupted vigilance* — what He's entrusted to us. This would be a good time to pause and ask yourself, *How well am I guarding and protecting my marriage? How can I come up higher and be more effective?*

As a Born-Again Believer You're a Supreme Champion!

Friend, God has made us an amazing promise in First John 5:4. He said, "For whatsoever is born of God overcometh the world: and this is the victory that overcometh the world, even our faith." Are you born of God? If you're a born-again believer, you, therefore, "overcometh the world"!

Notice the word "overcometh," which appears twice, and the word "victory." In all three instances, the words "overcometh" and "victory" are taken from the Greek word *nike*, which means *to conquer* or *to overcome.* This word was used to portray *athletes who gained the mastery in a competition and reigned supreme as champions over the games.* It pictures *ultimate champions* or *the superior position of an overcomer.*

Three times in this one verse, God declares you to be a superior champion — a conqueror who has gained a mastery position over the world — which in Greek refers to the systems of the world. How is this possible? It is through your faith! The more you yield to God's Spirit and develop your faith, the greater your ability will be to override whatever difficulty you're facing.

In our next lesson, we'll turn our attention to how we're to handle attacks against our children and grandchildren.

STUDY QUESTIONS

Study to shew thyself approved unto God, a workman that needeth not to be ashamed, rightly dividing the word of truth.
— 2 Timothy 2:15

1. Just how powerful are your words? The Bible says, "Death and life are in the power of the tongue…" (Proverbs 18:21), and each of us will be "…satisfied with the fruit of his mouth, and with the increase of his lips shall he be filled" (Proverbs 18:20). Take a look at these passages comparing *the mouth of the righteous* and *the mouth of a fool.* What are the differences?
   - **The Mouth of the Righteous** – Proverbs 10:11; Psalm 37:30,31; 1 Peter 2:22,23
   - **The Mouth of a Fool** – Proverbs 10:18; 15:2,4; 18:2,6,7,13; 20:3; 26:11

2. Knowing the great power of the words coming out of your mouth, how powerful do you think it is to use your mouth to speak God's Word? As you answer, consider Hebrews 4:12 and Jeremiah 5:14 and 23:28,29.

3. As a born-again believer, God declares you to be a supreme champion! How does Luke 10:19; Second Corinthians 2:14; and Romans 8:37 reaffirm this truth in First John5:4?

PRACTICAL APPLICATION

> But be ye doers of the word, and not hearers only,
> deceiving your own selves.
> — James 1:22

1. In what areas of your life do you need to get a better grip on your tongue? Where are you speaking words of fear, doubt, and negativity? What verses of truth can you find in Scripture to replace these *un*sound words and turn your mind and mouth into a powerhouse of health and productivity?

2. Christian marriages are a prime target of attack for the enemy. In what ways has Satan come against you and your spouse? What are some of the common thoughts he whispers to accuse your spouse to you in your mind? Have you ever had an open conversation with your spouse about these attacks from the enemy? Do you know what accusing thoughts he whispers to your spouse about you? If you'll expose his tactics to the light of truth, God will strengthen your relationship in ways you could never imagine. Try it and see!

3. Jesus and His disciples made it to the other side of the sea because Jesus stood up and took authority over the wind and the waves. Are you standing up and standing against the satanic attack that's been launched against you and your spouse? Are you speaking God's Word *over your marriage* and *against the enemy*? If you'll take authority over the devil and declare Truth, it's only a matter of time until his assault ceases!

LESSON 4

TOPIC

Attacks Against Your Children and Grandchildren

SCRIPTURES

1. **2 Timothy 1:11-14** — Whereunto I am appointed a preacher, and an apostle, and a teacher of the Gentiles. For the which cause I also

suffer these things: nevertheless I am not ashamed: for I know whom I have believed, and am persuaded that he is able to keep that which I have committed unto him against that day. Hold fast the form of sound words, which thou hast heard of me, in faith and love which is in Christ Jesus. That good thing which was committed unto thee keep by the Holy Ghost which dwelleth in us.

2. **1 Thessalonians 2:17,18** — But we, brethren, being taken from you for a short time in presence, not in heart, endeavoured the more abundantly to see your face with great desire. Wherefore we would have come unto you, even I, Paul, once and again; but Satan hindered us.

3. **2 Timothy 1:14** — That good thing which was committed unto thee keep by the Holy Ghost which dwelleth in us.

GREEK WORDS

1. "suffer" — **πάσχω** (*pasho*): I suffer; emotional suffering; strong feelings

2. "ashamed" — **ἐπαισχύνομαι** (*epaishunomai*): disgraced; put to shame; embarrassed; red-faced

3. "I know" — **οἶδα** (*oida*): to see, perceive, understand, or comprehend; knowledge gained by personal experience or personal observation

4. "persuaded" — **πείθω** (*peitho*): one who is convinced, coaxed, or swayed from one opinion to the opinion held by another; absolute confidence; convinced to the core; rock-solid certainty

5. "able" — **δυνατός** (*dunatos*): ability; power; a powerful force; amazing ability; to be able; capable or competent for any task; a force that causes one to be able or capable; one who is competent

6. "keep" — **φυλάσσω** (*phulasso*): to save, protect, preserve, or guard; a military guard who shows uninterrupted vigilance in guarding territory; the uninterrupted vigilance shepherds show in keeping their flocks

7. "committed" — **παραθήκη** (*paratheke*): entrust; deposit; commit into one's charge
or trust for safekeeping

8. "hold fast" — **ἔχε** (*eche*): to have, hold, retain, possess

9. "form" — **ὑποτύπωσις** (*hupotoposis*): compound of **ὑπό** (*hupo*) and **τύπος** (*tupos*); the word **ὑπό** (*hupo*) means by and the word **τύπος** (*tupos*) means a model or pattern; denotes a model forged by repetition; a pattern to be followed and repeated

10. "sound" — ὑγιαίνω (*hugiaino*): indicates something that is wholesome and healthy and that produces a healthy state of being
11. "Satan" — Σατανᾶς (*satanas*): one who hates, accuses, slanders, or conspires against
12. "hindered" — ἐγκόπτω (*egkopto*): to cut in on; to elbow out of the way; to block a road; to create an impasse; a disruption

SYNOPSIS

Leningrad is the old Soviet name for the modern city of Saint Petersburg, Russia. We have learned in our previous lessons that in 1941 Nazi troops surrounded this historic city in order to starve out its citizens and seize its control. To accomplish this, they formed a blockade which stopped virtually all food and supplies from entering the city. But the people of Leningrad were determined to maintain their territory at all costs.

The standoff lasted 900 days. During that hellacious timespan, food became so scarce that the people resorted to eating their pet dogs, cats, and birds. They even went so far as to eat the rats roaming the city as well as their own leather belts and shoes that they cooked. Imagine being a parent during this crisis and having to watch your children deal with such horrific conditions.

Amazingly, the city remained committed to functioning as normally as possible. This included the public school system continuing to teach children their scheduled studies. But the death grip of starvation brought about by the Nazi regime caused a number of children to perish right at their desks while they were in school. Still, the people of Leningrad held their ground and eventually outlasted the enemy.

Why did the Nazis want Leningrad so badly? It was a powerfully strategic stronghold for advancing their agenda of world domination. It's the same reason Satan attacks areas of our life. He's trying to establish a strategic stronghold from where he can totally dominate our every move. Many times our children end up in the crosshairs of his attack. He knows if he can take them down, he can greatly diminish our effectiveness — if not stop us all together.

If the enemy has come against your children or your grandchildren, don't give up hope! Instead, dig in your heels and stand your ground against the enemy! Your children and grandchildren have been entrusted to you from

God. Therefore, they are *your territory*, and Satan has no right to them. It's time to make the determination in faith that you're going to maintain the territory of your family. If you'll continue to stand in faith, God will turn it around!

The emphasis of this lesson:

Your children and grandchildren have been committed to you by God, and they are your responsibility. Just like your marriage and your finances, you are to save, protect, preserve, and guard them by the power of the Holy Spirit living in you. Rather than speak negatively, God wants you to speak words of life, love, and faith over your kids and grandkids and over your relationship with them.

A REVIEW OF OUR PREVIOUS LESSONS
Paul Was Suffering Because of His Calling

In Second Timothy 1:11, the apostle Paul writes, "Whereunto I am appointed a preacher, and an apostle, and a teacher of the Gentiles." Here Paul is really magnifying his call and his anointing from God. He then adds this statement in verse 12: "For the which cause I also suffer...." The Greek text actually says. "*For this very reason* I also suffer these things...."

The word "suffer" is the Greek word *pasho*, which means *I suffer*, and it can depict *physical suffering* or *emotional suffering*. Basically, Paul said, "I'm suffering things because I'm appointed as a preacher, an apostle, and teacher of the Gentiles. Who I am and what I'm doing has caused the devil to attack me relentlessly. He is threatened by me and the progress I'm making for the Kingdom of God." Indeed, when you know what God has called you to do and you begin to move in it, your obedience sometimes triggers an attack.

If you remember, Paul was suffering a bizarre attack. He had been arrested and thrown into prison in the city of Rome for a crime he never committed or had any part of. Meanwhile, the whole Roman Empire was talking about how bad he was, circulating slanderous allegations that were totally fabricated and unfounded.

Paul Was Not 'Ashamed'

To all this, Paul said, "...Nevertheless, I am not ashamed..." (2 Timothy 1:12). The Greek word for "ashamed" here is the equivalent of Paul saying, "I am *not disgraced*; I am *not put to shame*; and I am *not embarrassed.*" It literally means, "I am *not red-faced* and blushing with embarrassment." Paul knew who he was in Christ and who God was.

In fact, he said, "...For I know whom I have believed..." (2 Timothy 1:12). When Paul said, "I know," he used the Greek word *oida*, which means *to know by personal experience*. Paul had seen firsthand God's track record of faithfulness. He had walked long enough with the Lord that he knew God was in control, regardless of what things looked like in the natural.

Paul Was 'Persuaded'

Out of this deep knowing of God's dependability, Paul said, "...[I] am persuaded that he is able..." (2 Timothy 1:12). The word "persuaded" here is a translation of the Greek word *peitho*, and it describes *one who is convinced, one who is coaxed, or one who is swayed from one opinion to the opinion held by another.* This is a person who has been persuaded to the point of *absolute confidence*. They are *convinced to the core* with *rock-solid certainty*, and this persuasion is the result of intensive *self-talk*.

When we're going through difficult times, we all have moments when we open our mouths and begin to say negative things. Out of frustration and aggravation, we often speak words of doubt and fear, which are detrimental to our wellbeing. In those trying times we must realize, that a spirit of fear is trying to gain access into our life. Consequently, if we begin to speak fearful and doubtful words, we're actually partnering with and opening the door for the spirit of fear in our lives.

When Paul was in that dark, dank Roman prison, he more than likely had a bombardment of negative thoughts trying to land on the runway of his mind. It was in that crucial time he had to make a decision to speak the right kinds of words. Thus, in that cell all by himself, with no one around to encourage him, he made the decision to speak *positive, faith-filled* words to himself. He did such a thorough job of coaxing and convincing himself of God's goodness and power that he talked himself into a position of faith. This is a picture of "persuasion" – *peitho* — in action.

Paul Was Convinced of God's Ability To Keep Us

Paul said, "…[I] am persuaded that he is able…" (2 Timothy 1:12). The word "able" here is the Greek word *dunatos*, and it describes *ability, power,* or *a powerful force*. In this verse, it is describing God's *amazing power and ability*. Paul uses this word to demonstrate his belief that God is *a force that was well-able, capable, and competent* to "keep" him.

As we've noted, this word "keep" is a translation of the Greek word *phulasso*, which means *to save, protect, preserve, or guard*. Therefore, we could translate this part of Paul's declaration to say, "I am persuaded that God is able to *save* me, *protect* me, *preserve* me, and *guard* me." Interestingly, this word "keep" — the Greek word *phulasso* — was also used to describe *a military guard who used uninterrupted vigilance to guard territory that had been assigned to him*. It was also used to depict *shepherds who were keeping watch over and caring for their flocks with uninterrupted vigilance*.

Through the use of this word *phulasso*, translated "keep," Paul was declaring, "God is like a mighty, warring soldier watching over me and protecting me — His territory. He's my Good Shepherd, and I'm His sheep. He's guarding me and preserving my life with uninterrupted vigilance." That's exactly what God will do for you too as you commit your life into His safekeeping.

Paul Had 'Committed' Himself to God

What is God able to keep? Paul said, "…That which I have committed unto him against that day" (2 Timothy 1:12). The word "committed" here is the Greek word *paratheke*, and it means *to entrust* or *to deposit*. It is the picture of one *committing something into someone's charge or trust for safekeeping*.

In the same way money is placed into a night deposit box at a bank, when a person gives his life to Christ, he effectively *deposits* himself *in Christ* and is placed out of the enemy's reach. The moment he or she is *in Christ*, nothing and no one can tamper with or touch him or her. This is what the apostle Paul was saying. He believed beyond the shadow of a doubt that God was able to keep him until "that day," which refers to the day we see Jesus face-to-face and our mission here is completed.

We Are To 'Hold Fast'
the Form of Sound Words

Paul went on to tell Timothy, "Hold fast the form of sound words, which thou hast heard of me, in faith and love which is in Christ Jesus" (2 Timothy 1:13). The words "hold fast" are from the Greek word *eche*, which means *to have, hold, retain, or possess*. The implication here is that if we don't make a concerted, determined effort to hold onto and retain the form of sound words, they are going to slip away from us.

What did Paul mean when he referred to "the form of sound words"? Well, the Greek word for "form" is *hupotoposis*, which is a compound of the words *hupo* and *tupos*. The word *hupo* means *by*, and the word *tupos* describes *a model* or *pattern* that has been *forged by repetition*. It is *a pattern to be followed and repeated*. In this case, the *pattern* Paul was telling Timothy to follow and repeat was the pattern of "sound words" Paul had modeled in front of him.

The word "sound" here is the Greek word *hugiaino*, and it signifies *anything that is wholesome, healthy, and produces a healthy state of being*. The fact is, some words we speak produce life, peace, faith, and victory. Then there are other words we speak that generate fear, doubt, hopelessness, and defeat. Paul was writing to Timothy at a time he was being tempted to give into fear and to begin speaking negativity. Basically, Paul urged him to get a grip on his words.

That's what Paul meant when he said, "Hold fast the form of sound words, which thou hast heard of me, in faith and love which is in Christ Jesus" (2 Timothy 1:13). This was the equivalent of Paul saying, "Hey Timothy, you know how I talk, so talk like me. Repeat the kind of faith-filled words and phrases you've heard me say again and again when we were going through hardships together. Monitor your mouth, and stick with the pattern I showed you. Speak *sound* words, not negative or fearful words. Talk about what is *wholesome, healthy*, and what will produce *a healthy state of being*."

Remember, *we get what we say, so say what you want to see*. When you're being attacked, speak words of *faith* and not fear. If you speak negative words of fear and unbelief, you will cooperate with what the spirit of fear is trying to produce in your life. On the other hand, when you speak *sound* words of faith and love, you will be cooperating with the Holy Spirit so that He can bring about God's good plan for your life.

Your Children and Grandchildren Have Been Committed to You by God

Immediately after Paul urged Timothy to get a grip on the words of his mouth, he said, "That good thing which was committed unto thee keep by the Holy Ghost which dwelleth in us" (2 Timothy 1:14). Just as your marriage, the calling on your life, and the anointing of the Holy Spirit have been committed to you, so have your children and grandchildren. They are another "good thing" God has entrusted to you.

Your children and grandchildren are your responsibility regardless of their age. Obviously, when they're younger, the full weight of responsibility for their lives rests on you. As they get older, your responsibility shifts to being a source of wise, godly counsel and providing a solid, ongoing prayer covering for them.

Unfortunately, sometimes there is a disruption and a separation that occurs between us and our children as they grow up, and when that occurs it is very hurtful and unpleasant. In situations like these, we often don't know what to do to see a loving connection restored. The longer the breach lasts, the more we're tempted to say all the negative things we feel inside. In times like these, we need to follow Paul's instruction and *hold fast to sound words*. We need to get a grip on the words of our lips and speak every good thing we can think of about our kids and grandkids.

Satan Conspires Against Us Using Accusations and Slander

The apostle Paul experienced a major disruption in his relationship with the believers in Thessalonica. In many ways, they were like his spiritual children, and he was like their spiritual father. He loved them and he longed to be with them and see their faces. We see this in First Thessalonians 2:17 and 18, where he said:

> But we, brethren, being taken from you for a short time in presence, not in heart, endeavoured the more abundantly to see your face with great desire. Wherefore we would have come unto you, even I, Paul, once and again; but Satan hindered us.

Notice the word "Satan" in this verse. It is a translation of the Greek word *satanas*, which describes *one who hates, accuses, slanders, or conspires against*.

Again, these Thessalonian believers were like spiritual children to Paul, and Satan had slithered his way in between him and them and began to bring a disruption to their relationship.

In the same way, Satan often comes between us and our children and our grandchildren, whispering thoughts of slander and accusation to bring about separation. He hates and despises your relationships with your offspring and is relentlessly working to conspire against you and disrupt your relationships.

In Paul's situation, he said, "…Satan hindered us" (1 Thessalonians 2:18). That word "hindered" is the Greek word *egkopto*, and it means *to cut in on*. That is what the devil is constantly trying to do — *to cut in on* your relationship with your kids and grandkids.

This word *egkopto* — translated here as "hindered" — also means *to elbow out of the way*. This is the very word that was used to depict a runner who is running in a race and doing very well, but suddenly another runner comes up alongside him and begins to use his elbow to push the other runner out of the way. Likewise, that is what the devil wants to do with you and your offspring. He wants to elbow you right out of relationship with them.

Furthermore, the word *egkopto* ("hindered") can also mean *to block a road*, *create an impasse*, or *bring a disruption*. Honestly, there are few disruptions more unpleasant than the one that occurs between a parent and his or her children or grandchildren. It is such a disturbing impasse we often don't know how to get through it. As the hurt and discomfort mount inside us, we often begin to speak every fearful and foul thing we feel.

Again, these kinds of words serve only to empower Satan's work in the situation and make matters worse. This is why we need to learn to get a grip on what we're saying. Remember, "Death and life are in the power of the tongue…" (Proverbs 18:21). It's time to begin using your tongue to speak words of life, love, and faith over your children and grandchildren and over our relationships with them.

Protect, Preserve, and Guard Your Kids and Grandkids By the Power of the Holy Spirit

Looking once more at Paul's charge in Second Timothy 1:14, he said, "That good thing which was committed unto thee *keep* by the Holy Ghost which dwelleth in us." There are so many wonderful things God has committed to you, and among them are your children and grandchildren. He has instructed you to "keep" them, and this word "keep" is again a form of the Greek word *phulasso*, and it means *to save, protect, preserve, or guard.* It depicts *a military guard who shows uninterrupted vigilance in guarding territory,* and it also denotes *the uninterrupted vigilance shepherds show in keeping their flocks.*

Friend, just as God has promised to "keep" (*phulasso*) you, He wants you to "keep" your kids and grandkids. He wants you to *save, protect, preserve, and guard them with uninterrupted vigilance.* They are your territory — they are your flock to watch over and care for. If it seems there's been a disruption or you've reached an impasse in your relationship, then begin to cover and hover over them in prayer. Monitor your mouth and make sure you're speaking positive words of faith, hope, and love. Be willing to forgive and let go of past hurts.

"How in the world can I do all that?" you ask. Paul said, "…By the Holy Ghost which dwelleth in us" (2 Timothy 1:14). Again, the word "dwelleth" here means *to take up permanent residence.* That is what the Holy Spirit does the day you surrender your life to the lordship of Jesus — He becomes a *permanent resident* inside you, which means you're not alone! You have the supernatural partnership of the Holy Spirit living inside you! He will empower you to do everything you need to do — including what it takes to "keep" your children and grandchildren.

In our final lesson, we will turn our attention to how to handle the enemy's attacks against our health.

STUDY QUESTIONS

Study to shew thyself approved unto God, a workman that needeth not to be ashamed, rightly dividing the word of truth.
— 2 Timothy 2:15

1. Have you ever experienced a time when it seemed you just didn't like your child or grandchild — when all you could see or think about were their faults and mistakes? Don't be alarmed. This is a strategy of Satan to steal, kill, and destroy your child's destiny. To turn the tables, pray for God to give you *eyes* to see and *ears* to hear what you can't see and hear in the natural. Ask Him to reveal the hidden treasures He

has placed in your children/grandchildren and begin to call into existence those things that don't exist as though they did! (*See* Romans 4:17.)

2. Philippians 4:8 (*TLB*) says, "…Fix your thoughts on what is true and good and right. Think about things that are pure and lovely, and dwell on the fine, good things in others…." To help you practice this, make a list of every good quality your children/grandchildren have that you can think of, and thank God for these good things in their lives.

PRACTICAL APPLICATION

But be ye doers of the word, and not hearers only,
deceiving your own selves.
—James 1:22

1. Has there been a disruption or separation between you and your children or grandchildren? If so, what happened that caused the breach to occur? How is the enemy working to elbow you out of relationship with your kids and grandkids?

2. Have you been tempted to speak mean, negative words to them or about them? If you've given into that temptation, pray and ask God to forgive you for the words you've spoken. If you've said hurtful things to your children or grandchildren, pray for the right timing and the right words to sincerely apologize to them.

3. In your personal prayer time, begin to regularly cover your children and grandchildren — and your relationship with them — in prayer. Speak the Word over them and over your relationship. Here is a sample prayer to help you begin:

Father, thank You for [insert children's names]. *I cover them and our relationship with the precious blood of Jesus. I declare that no weapon formed against them will prosper* (see Isaiah 54:17). *I stand against and bind up every evil spirit of rebellion, anger, strife, offense, lies, and deception and cast them away from my kids* (see Matthew 16:19; 18:18). *I loose your love, joy, peace, truth, and reconciliation in all our lives. Give me eyes to see them the way You see them. Melt the hardness off their heart and my heart and heal the hurts we have caused each other. I bless my relationship with* [insert children's names] *with love, peace, honesty, trust, and laughter. I ask and declare these things in the mighty name of Jesus. Amen!*

TOPIC

Attacks Against Your Health

SCRIPTURES

1. **2 Timothy 1:11-14** — Whereunto I am appointed a preacher, and
   an apostle, and a teacher of the Gentiles. For the which cause I also
   suffer these things: nevertheless I am not ashamed: for I know whom
   I have believed, and am persuaded that he is able to keep that which
   I have committed unto him against that day. Hold fast the form of
   sound words, which thou hast heard of me, in faith and love which is
   in Christ Jesus. That good thing which was committed unto thee keep
   by the Holy Ghost which dwelleth in us.

2. **Philippians 2:25-27** — Yet I supposed it necessary to send to you
   Epaphroditus, my brother, and companion in labour, and fellow-
   soldier, but your messenger, and he that ministered to my wants. For
   he longed after you all, and was full of heaviness, because that ye had
   heard that he had been sick. For indeed he was sick nigh unto death:
   but God had mercy on him; and not on him only, but on me also, lest
   I should have sorrow upon sorrow.

3. **2 Timothy 1:14** — That good thing which was committed unto thee
   keep by the Holy Ghost which dwelleth in us.

4. **1 John 5:4** — For whatsoever is born of God overcometh the world:
   and this is the victory that overcometh the world, even our faith.

GREEK WORDS

1. "suffer" — πάσχω (*pasho*): I suffer; emotional suffering; strong feelings

2. "ashamed" — ἐπαισχύνομαι (*epaishunomai*): disgraced; put to shame;
   embarrassed; red-faced

3. "I know" — οἶδα (*oida*): to see, perceive, understand, or comprehend;
   knowledge gained by personal experience or personal observation

4. "persuaded" — πείθω (*peitho*): one who is convinced, coaxed, or
   swayed from one opinion to the opinion held by another; absolute
   confidence; convinced to the core; rock-solid certainty

5. "able" — δυνατός (*dunatos*): ability; power; a powerful force; amazing ability; to be able; capable or competent for any task; a force that causes one to be able or capable; one who is competent

6. "keep" — φυλάσσω (*phulasso*): to save, protect, preserve, or guard; a military guard who shows uninterrupted vigilance in guarding territory; the uninterrupted vigilance shepherds show in keeping their flocks

7. "committed" — παραθήκη (*paratheke*): entrust; deposit; commit into one's charge or trust for safekeeping

8. "hold fast" — ἔχε (*eche*): to have, hold, retain, possess

9. "form" — ὑποτύπωσις (*hupotoposis*): compound of ὑπό (*hupo*) and τύπος (*tupos*); the word ὑπό (*hupo*) means by and the word τύπος (*tupos*) means a model or pattern; denotes a model forged by repetition; a pattern to be followed and repeated

10. "sound" — ὑγιαίνω (*hugiaino*): indicates something that is wholesome and healthy and that produces a healthy state of being

11. "sick" — ἀσθενέω (*astheneo*): describes a person who is frail in health; people so physically weak that they were unable to travel; it carries the idea of those who were feeble, fragile, faint, incapacitated, disabled, or simply in such poor health that it would be unthinkable to transport them; shut-ins or homebound; can also mean to be in financial need

12. "nigh unto" — παραπλήσιον (*paraplesion*): compound of παρά (*para*) and πλησίον (*plesion*); the word (*para*) means alongside of; near; the word πλησίον (*plesion*) is the word for a neighbor or one that is nearby or neighboring; compounded, very near, in close proximity

13. "death" — θάνατος (*thanatos*): physical or spiritual death; it can mean mortal danger or a dangerous circumstance

14. "mercy" — ἔλεος (*eleos*): pity; compassion; deep-seated and unsettling emotions a person feels in response to something seen or heard; a heart-wrenching emotion that compels one to action

15. "committed" — παραθήκη (*paratheke*): entrusted; deposited; committed into one's charge or trust for safekeeping

SYNOPSIS

How important is your health to God? It is very important! Through the apostle John, He tells us, "…I pray that you may enjoy good health and that all may go well with you, even as your soul is getting along well"

(3 John 2 *NIV*). Indeed, our God is the God who *heals* (*see* Exodus 15:26). The psalmist declared, "God spoke the words 'Be healed,' and we were healed, delivered from death's door!" (Psalm 107:20 *TPT*).

Make no mistake: God wants you to be healthy and healed. It is the enemy that wants you sick. Just as the enemy attacks your finances, your marriage, and your relationships, he sometimes attacks your health. What are you to do if you've done everything you know to do to be healthy and you still get sick? That's one of the questions we'll answer in this lesson.

The emphasis of this lesson:

Your body is the temple of the Holy Spirit, and in order for you to be most effective for the Kingdom of God, you need to be in good health. Satan will sometimes attack the health of good, godly people just like he did in the case of Epaphroditus. If you're suffering physically and your health is under attack, God wants to take action and release healing into your life.

A FINAL REVIEW OF OUR ANCHOR VERSE
2 Timothy 1:12

When Paul wrote his second letter to his spiritual son Timothy, he began by talking about the magnificent work of Christ and how He abolished death and "brought life and immortality to light through the gospel" (2 Timothy 1:10). It was for this glorious gospel that Paul said, "Whereunto I am appointed a preacher, and an apostle, and a teacher of the Gentiles" (2 Timothy 1:11).

Then in the next verse he said, "For the which cause I also suffer these things…" (2 Timothy 1:12). This was the equivalent of Paul saying, "If you want to know why I'm having all the trouble I'm having, it's because I've been appointed a preacher, an apostle, and a teacher of the Gentiles. That's the reason I'm suffering in this prison."

The word "suffer" in verse 12 is the Greek word *pasho*, which means *to physically suffer* or *emotionally suffer*. At this particular moment in Paul's life, he had been arrested and incarcerated in a Roman prison for a crime he didn't commit. He had been falsely accused of arson and was said to have been behind a master plan to burn down the central section of Rome. This fake news report was spread throughout the city, causing many to believe Paul was a notorious criminal that deserved imprisonment — or even death.

Clearly, the call on Paul's life was God-ordained, and the devil was after him to put a stop to his efforts. It was this divine call — and the great success Paul was experiencing — that triggered the enemy's attack.

Amazingly, in the midst of ongoing suffering, Paul declared:

> **...Nevertheless I am not ashamed: for I know whom I have believed, and am persuaded that he is able to keep that which I have committed unto him against that day.**
> **— 2 Timothy 1:12**

Paul said, "...I am not ashamed..." (2 Timothy 1:12). The word "ashamed" here is the Greek word *epaishunomai*, which means *to be disgraced, put to shame*, or *embarrassed*. This word depicts *one who is so embarrassed their face is turning red*. In Paul's case, he was *not* disgraced or embarrassed or red in the face. Despite the fact he was in prison and being lied about by the Roman officials, he was not ashamed. Why? It's because he knew who he was. He had learned to turn a deaf ear to the opinions and criticism of others. Likewise, Paul also knew in whom he was believing.

Paul said, "...For I know whom I have believed..." (2 Timothy 1:12). In Greek, the phrase "I know" is the word *oida*, which means *to see, perceive, understand, or comprehend*. It denotes *knowledge gained by personal experience* or *personal observation*. By this point in Paul's life, he had enough personal experience with God to know He is in control. That's one of the greatest benefits of walking with the Lord. The longer you're in relationship with Him and personally experience His goodness and faithfulness, the more confidence and faith you have in Him.

Paul said, "...[I] am persuaded..." (2 Timothy 1:12). The word "persuaded" here is the Greek word *peitho*, and it describes *one who is convinced, coaxed, or swayed from one opinion to the opinion held by another*. The use of this word (*peitho*) tells us Paul had to be coaxed and swayed from one thought to another thought. Remember, Paul was suffering in a deplorable Roman prison — a place where most prisoners ended up dying.

In that dark, desperate dungeon, he was probably dealing with many fearful, negative thoughts.

But rather than give place to those thoughts and the evil spirits behind them, Paul began to talk to himself, coaxing and convincing himself that God was still with him and that He would be faithful to take care of him. That is what this word *peitho* describes — *self-persuasion*. Paul talked himself out of a position of doubt and fear and into a position of faith and hope.

When you find yourself in a dark, difficult place, you need to begin to talk to yourself and remind yourself of God's goodness and all the times He has provided and protected you in the past. Your ears believe what your voice says. If you speak words of faith and hope to yourself, you will believe what you hear. Paul talked to himself and persuaded himself to stay in a place of faith. He became *convinced to the core* with *rock-solid certainty* that God was able to keep him.

Paul said, "...He is able to keep..." (2 Timothy 1:12). The word "able" here is the Greek word *dunatos*, and it describes *ability, power,* or *a powerful force.* It is a picture of one with *amazing ability* or *one who is able, capable, or competent for any task.* By using this word "keep" (*dunatos*), Paul was saying, "God is absolutely *competent* and *capable* to 'keep' me through this extremely difficult situation."

The word "keep" here is a form of the Greek word *phulasso*, which means *to save, protect, preserve, or guard.* Hence, Paul was saying, "God is well-able to *save* me, *protect* me, *preserve* me, and *guard* me." This word *phulasso* — translated here as "keep" — was also used to depict *a military guard who displayed uninterrupted vigilance in guarding territory.* Additionally, it depicted *the uninterrupted vigilance shepherds showed in keeping their flocks.* By using this word, Paul was saying, "God is my Mighty Warrior, and I am the territory He is assigned to guard. He is my Great Shepherd, and I am His sheep He is watching over and caring for. I'm fully convinced that He is competent and capable to protect and preserve me with uninterrupted vigilance."

What is God able to keep? Paul said, "...That which I have committed unto him against that day" (2 Timothy 1:12). The word "committed" in this verse is the Greek word *paratheke*, which is a compound of the words *para* and a form of the word *tithimi.* The word *para* means *alongside,* and the word *tithimi* means *to place, to lay down,* or *to deposit.* When these words are compounded to form *paratheke*, it means *to entrust* or *to deposit*. It depicts *coming alongside something and committing something into one's charge or trust for safekeeping*.

By using this word *paratheke* ("committed"), Paul likened himself to money placed into a night depository at a bank. Once that deposit is placed into the small opening and the metal door is pulled closed, the deposit is safely secured inside the bank and cannot be touched or tampered with in any way. In the same way, when we give our lives to Jesus, we place ourselves *in Christ*. We are now safe and secure in His keeping.

That is what Paul meant when he said he had "committed" himself to God against that day. He knew that no one could touch or harm him because he was locked up *in Jesus Christ* forever. The words "that day" refer to the day we see Jesus face to face and our mission here is fulfilled.

Having Good Health Is Vital

One of the most important things that each of us needs to commit to the Lord is our health. Again and again we are told that our body is the temple of the Holy Spirit (*see* 1 Corinthians 6:19), and in order for us to be most effective for the Kingdom of God, we need to be in good health. We have a part to play, and God has a part to play. Our part is to eat right, drink an adequate amount of water, exercise, get proper rest, and use wisdom to reduce stress in our life.

Unfortunately, there are many people — including many Christians — who have poor health because they have made poor choices and not taken good care of themselves. Let's face it: a steady diet of junk foods, sugary drinks, lack of water, no exercise, and insufficient sleep is an open door for sickness and disease to enter. God has given us a mind and will, and He wants us to use them to make smart, healthy choices that produce life.

Of course, there are situations where a person is doing all the right things, and they still end up getting sick. This is the result of a direct assault from the enemy. Jesus made it clear that Satan is a thief, and, "The thief cometh not, but for to steal, and to kill, and destroy…" (John 10:10). Thankfully, Jesus didn't stop there but went on to add in the same verse, "…I am come that they might have life, and that they might have it more abundantly."

Sometimes Good, Godly People
Are Attacked With Sickness

There's an interesting story Paul shares in his letter to the Philippians about a believer who was attacked with sickness. He said, "Yet I supposed it necessary to send to you Epaphroditus, my brother, and companion in labour, and fellowsoldier, but your messenger, and he that ministered to my wants" (Philippians 2:25). Clearly, Epaphroditus was a very special friend to Paul. Not only was he his "fellow-soldier" in the sharing of the Gospel, Paul also called him his "brother" and one that personally ministered to his "wants."

Paul went on to say, "For he [Epaphroditus] longed after you all, and was full of heaviness, because that ye had heard that he had been sick" (Philippians 2:26). Please don't miss this important point: Epaphroditus was not a nobody. He was a cherished servant with significant ministry status. Paul described him as a *brother*, a *companion in labor*, a *fellow soldier*, and a *messenger*. What's interesting is that this word "messenger" is the Greek word *apostolos*, which is the word for an *apostle*. Therefore, Epaphroditus stood in the office of an *apostle*.

Yet in spite of his high status and the excellence in which he served in ministry, he still got sick. This lets us know that sickness knows no boundaries. Satan will sometimes attack the health of good, godly people just like he did in the case of Epaphroditus.

The word "sick" in Philippians 2:26 is the Greek word *astheneo*, and it describes *a person who is frail in health* or *one who is so physically weak that they were unable to travel*. It carries the idea of those who were *feeble, fragile, faint, incapacitated, disabled*, or simply *in such poor health that it would be unthinkable to transport them*. Thus, the word *astheneo* — translated here as "sick" — depicts *shut-ins* or *those who are homebound*.

Interestingly, this word can also mean *to be in financial need*, which is significant, because when you've been stricken in your physical health, it very often affects your finances. You're spending money on medication, doctor visits, and possibly hospitalization. And because of your compromised health, you are often not able to work. Hence, sickness is a major attack of the enemy that affects not only your body, but also your finances, your social status, and your relationships.

How Sick Was Epaphroditus?

Paul tells us in Philippians 2:27: "For indeed he was sick nigh unto death…." Notice the words "nigh unto." It is the Greek word *paraplesion*, which is a compound of the words *para* and *plesion*. The word *para* means *alongside of* or *near*, and the word *plesion* is the word for *a neighbor* or *one that is nearby or neighboring*. When these words are compounded to form *paraplesion*, it means *very near, in close proximity*.

Paul said Epaphroditus was nigh unto "death," which is the Greek word *thanatos*, and it describes *physical or spiritual death*. It can also denote *mortal danger* or *a dangerous circumstance*. Therefore, when Paul said Epaphroditus "…was sick nigh unto death…," it was the same as him saying, "Epaphroditus was living next door to death." That's how critically ill he was.

Thankfully the story doesn't end there. Paul went on to say, "…But God had mercy on him; and not on him only, but on me also, lest I should have sorrow upon sorrow" (Philippians 2:27). The word "mercy" here is the Greek word *eleos*, and it describes *pity* or *compassion*. This is *deep-seated and unsettling emotions a person feels in response to something seen or heard*. Furthermore, this word "mercy" (*eleos*) indicates *a heart-wrenching emotion that compels one to action*.

The use of this word tells us clearly that God didn't just see Epaphroditus and say, "Aw, poor Epaphroditus. I'm so sad that he's sick and I hope he gets better." On the contrary, God's *mercy* and compassion drove Him to take action on Epaphroditus' behalf, causing Him to step in and heal Epaphroditus completely.

Friend, please know that if God sees you are suffering physically and that your health is under an attack, He wants to take action and move on your behalf. His compassion always results in action, but you have to release your faith and cooperate with the work of His Holy Spirit in your life.

God Has Entrusted Your Health to You and His Spirit Will Empower You to 'Keep' It

Turning our attention once more to Paul's charge in Second Timothy 1:14, he said, "That good thing which was committed unto thee keep by the Holy Ghost which dwelleth in us." Like your marriage, your finances, and your children, your *health* is one more "good thing" God has "committed" to you. Again, this word "committed" is the Greek word *paratheke*, which means *entrusted, deposited*, or *committed into one's charge or trust for safekeeping*.

God has entrusted your health into your safekeeping. He is calling on you to "keep" your health, just as you're to "keep" every other "good thing" He has deposited in your life. Again, this word "keep" is a form of the Greek word *phulasso*, and it means *to save, protect, preserve, or guard*. It depicts *a military guard who shows uninterrupted vigilance in guarding territory*, and it also denotes *the uninterrupted vigilance shepherds show in keeping their flocks*.

Friend, just as God has promised to "keep" (*phulasso*) you, He wants you to "keep" your health. To the best of your ability, He wants you to *protect, preserve, and guard your health with uninterrupted vigilance*. Your health is your territory, and you are to watch over and care for it. How? Paul said, "…By the Holy Ghost which dwelleth in us" (2 Timothy 1:14). Remember, the Holy Spirit has taken up *permanent residency* inside you. He's your supernatural partner supplying you with supernatural power! He is ready, willing, and able to help you walk in divine health.

God's merciful compassion is moving in your direction in this moment. To receive it, reach out in faith and say, "Lord, I receive Your healing power right now. Thank You for helping me develop the discipline I need to get back into good physical shape. In Jesus' name. Amen!"

STUDY QUESTIONS

> Study to shew thyself approved unto God, a workman that
> needeth not to be ashamed, rightly dividing the word of truth.
> — 2 Timothy 2:15

1. If you are battling sickness or disease, it is vital for you to know two things: *God is willing to heal you* and *He is able to heal you*. Take time to carefully meditate on these promises He made to you and begin to speak them out over your life.

   • **The Lord wants to heal you:** Matthew 8:1-3; Mark 1:40-42; Luke 5:12,13; 3 John 2

   • **Through Jesus you are healed:** Matthew 8:17; Isaiah 53:4,5; 1 Peter 2:24

- **God is well-able to heal you:** Matthew 19:26; Luke 1:37; Jeremiah 32:27; Ephesians 3:20

2. Sometimes when physical illness lingers, we begin to wonder if it's something we've done to open the door to the enemy. If this is a question you have, pray and ask God to show you the truth. If you've done (or failed to do) something that has opened the door to sickness, *repent* and ask God to forgive you and give you the grace to make the right changes. Whether He shows you something or not, know that *you are loved by God*, and He is not punishing you. Take time to look up and carefully meditate on these verses, making them a declaration of faith for your healing.

   - **Jesus came to give you life, not sickness and disease:** John 10:10; Romans 6:4,5

   - **Through Jesus' finished work, you share His nature:** 2 Peter 1:3,4; Colossians 2:9,10

   - **Feed on the Word; it produces health and healing:** Proverbs 4:20-22; Psalm 107:20

   - **Feed on fellowship with Christ Himself; His presence is life giving:** John 6:48-58,63

PRACTICAL APPLICATION

But be ye doers of the word, and not hearers only,
deceiving your own selves.
—James 1:22

1. There are many people — including many Christians — who have poor health because they have made poor choices and not taken good care of themselves. Be honest: Does this describe you? Are you eating right, exercising, and getting proper rest? Or have you really let yourself go?

2. When it comes to improving your health, what do you know in your heart you need to change? What has God been prompting you to do differently — regarding eating, sleeping, exercise, and reducing stress?

3. Sickness is a major attack of the enemy that affects not only your body, but also your finances, your social status, and your relationships. Are you or someone close to you battling sickness of some kind?

www.ingramcontent.com/pod-product-compliance
Lightning Source LLC
Chambersburg PA
CBHW051047030426

42339CB00006B/242